Songs We Love To Sing

BOOK 1

The Mike Sammes Choral Favourites Series

Kevin Mayhew

We hope you enjoy the music in this book.
Further copies are available from your local music shop.

In case of difficulty, please contact the publisher direct by writing to:

The Sales Department
KEVIN MAYHEW LTD
Rattlesden
Bury St Edmunds
Suffolk
IP30 0SZ

Phone 01449 737978
Fax 01449 737834

Please ask for our complete catalogue of outstanding Vocal Music.

Acknowledgements

The Publishers wish to express their gratitude to the following for
permission to include copyright material in this book:

Barry Mason Enterprises Ltd, 22 Priory Terrace, London NW6 4DH
for *So in love with you* © Barry Mason Enterprises.

Cyril Shane Music Ltd, Suite 8, Westmead House, Westmead Road, Sutton,
Surrey SM1 4JH for *A Little Knowledge* © Pedro Music Ltd, rights assigned to
Cyril Shane Music Ltd, and *The Great Gnome Robbery* © Cyril Shane Music Ltd.

First published in Great Britain in 1996 by Kevin Mayhew Ltd.

© Copyright 1996 Kevin Mayhew Ltd.

ISBN 0 86209 744 4
Catalogue No: 3611195

The texts and music in this book are protected by copyright and may not be reproduced
in any way for sale or private use without the consent of the copyright owner.

Front Cover: *The Rehearsal* by Pieter Jacobs Codde (1599-1678).
Reproduced by courtesy of Baumkotter Gallery/Fine Art Photographic Library, London.
Cover design by Graham Johnstone and Veronica Ward.

Music Editors: Stephanie Hill and Donald Thomson
Music setting by Tracy Cracknell

Printed and bound in Great Britain

Contents

	Page
A little knowledge	72
Comin' through the rye	54
Humming Bird	46
I know where I'm goin'	18
Michael, row the boat ashore	5
So in love with you	26
Soldier, soldier	80
The Great Gnome Robbery	33
The Kerry Dance	64
The Virgin Mary	92
Versatility	43

MIKE SAMMES is the founder of the famous Mike Sammes Singers, who have worked with hundreds of major artists including Cliff Richard, Andy Williams, The Beatles, Tom Jones, Barbara Streisand – the list is endless. They have also issued a string of successful solo albums of their own and were recently awarded BASCA's Gold Badge for services to British music.

MICHAEL, ROW THE BOAT ASHORE

Text: Traditional American
Music: Traditional American Melody arranged by Mike Sammes

*Finger clicks on the off beats

© Copyright 1996 Kevin Mayhew Ltd.
It is illegal to photocopy music.

6

21
hal - le - lu - ia,
help to trim the sails,
24
Sis - ter, help to trim the sails, hal - le - lu - ia.
28
S
A
Mi - chael, row the boat a - shore, hal - le -
T
B

lu - ia, Mi - chael, row the boat a - shore, ha - le - lu - ia.

The river Jordan is chilly and cold, hallelujah, chills the body but not the soul, hallelujah. Michael, row the boat a-shore, hal-le-lu-ia, Mi-chael, row the boat a-shore, hal-le-lu-ia.

58
mf
dool yup dt dt do dt do,
mf
62
do ba do 'n do dool yup do 'n do dt.
f
66
Spoken firmly
niet!
3

Come on, an' row that boat a-shore, the ri-ver is deep and the ri-ver is wide, milk and ho-ney on the o-ther side,

13

89
row, row, row, hal - le - lu - ia, row that boat a-shore,
92
row, row, row, hal - le - lu - ia,
95
row that boat a - shore! Row, row, row,

98
hal - le - lu - ia, row that boat a - shore.
101
Row, row, row, hal - le - lu - ia, row that boat a - shore.
104
mp
Mi - chael, row the boat a - shore, hal - le - lu - ia,
mp
mp

*Finger clicks on the off beats

row that boat a-shore, Mi-chael, row that boat a-shore,

hal - le - lu -

ia, come on row that boat a-shore!

ff

17

I KNOW WHERE I'M GOIN'

Text: Traditional Irish
Music: Traditional Irish Melody arranged by Mike Sammes

© Copyright 1996 Kevin Mayhew Ltd.
It is illegal to photocopy music.

11

I know who I love, but the dear knows who I'll mar-ry. I have stock-ings of silk, I have stock-ings of silk, shoes of fine green lea-ther, combs to bu-ckle my shoes of fine green lea-ther,

hair and a ring for ev-'ry fin-ger.
combs for her hair and a ring for ev-'ry fin-ger.

*Swing a bit

S Some say he's black, but
A Some say he's black, but
T Some say he's black, but
B Some say he's black, but

Play dotted rhythms as triplets

I say he's bon-ny, the fair-est of them all,
I say he's bon-ny, the fair-est of them all,
I say he's bon-ny, the fair-est of them all,
I say he's bon-ny, the fair-est of them all,

my hand-some, win-some John-ny,
my hand-some, win-some John-ny,
my hand-some, win-some John-ny,
my hand-some, win-some John-ny,

35
mp
Fea - ther beds are
Fea - ther beds are
Fea - ther beds are
Fea - ther beds are

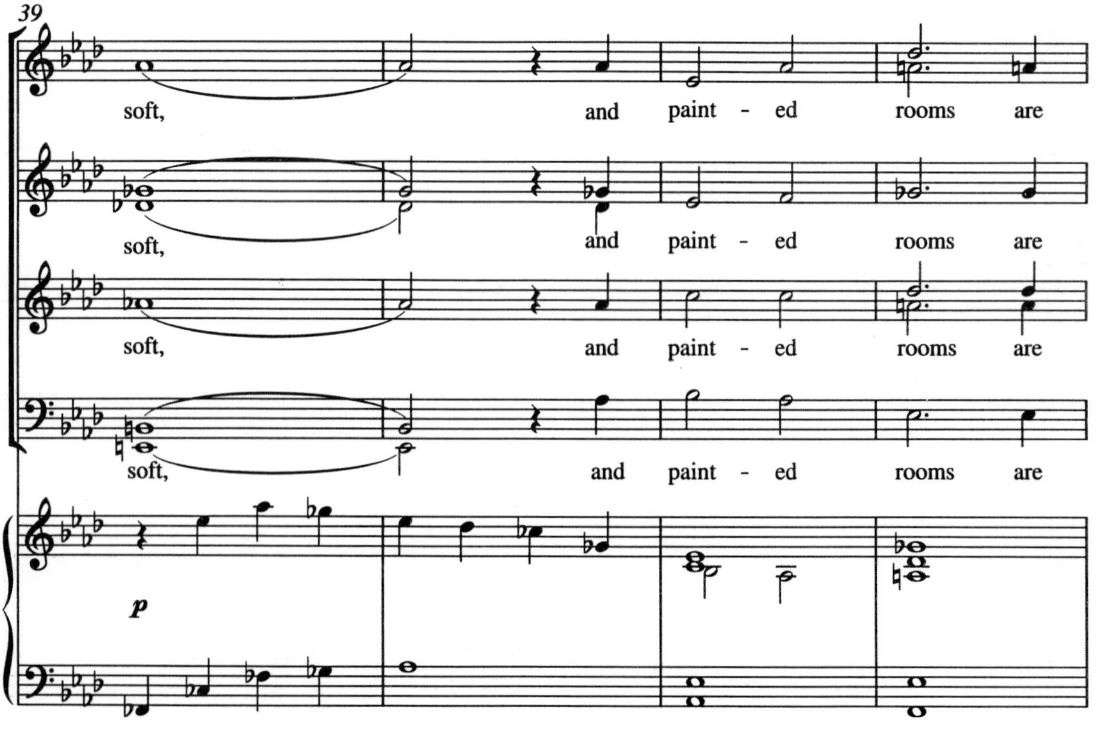
39
soft, and paint - ed rooms are
soft, and paint - ed rooms are
soft, and paint - ed rooms are
soft, and paint - ed rooms are
p

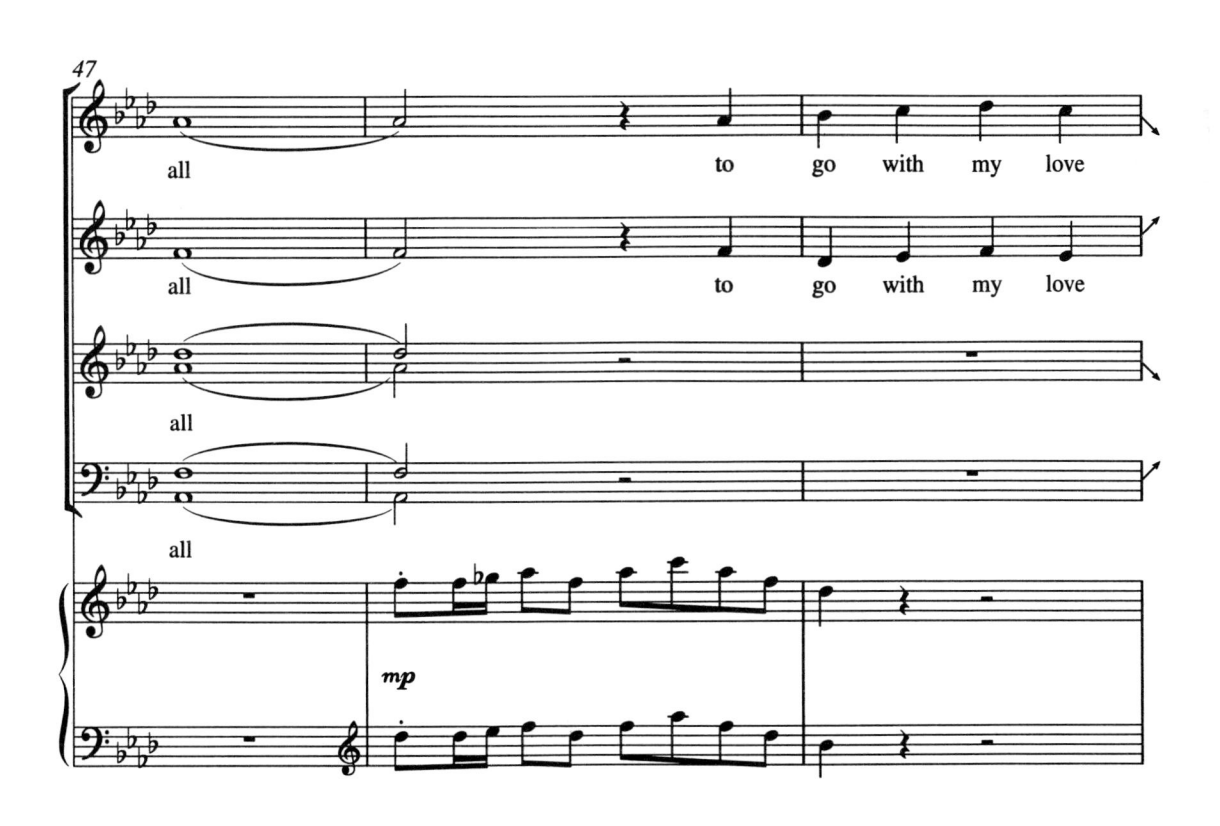

bon - ny, but I would leave them
bon - ny, but I would leave them
bon - ny, but I would leave them
bon - ny, but I would leave them

all to go with my love
all to go with my love
all
all

mp

50
S
A
John - ny.
T
B
sedately
53
I know where I'm go - in' and I know who's go - in'
56
rit.
mp
with me, I know who I love, but the
mp
rit.

dear knows who I'll mar - ry.

I know where I'm go - in'.

SO IN LOVE WITH YOU

Text: Barry Mason
Music: Léo Delibes arranged by Mike Sammes

Lyrics:

At the end of the day, for a moment or two, all my thoughts fly away, as I sit here with you, to the

* Play dotted rhythm as triplets

© Copyright Barry Mason Enterprises, 22 Priory Terrace, London NW6 4DH. Reproduced by permission.
It is illegal to photocopy music.

thrills and de-lights of those long sum-mer nights when life and love was new.

I can still see you there, look-ing shy and a-lone, till we

Ooh,

27

ooh, it was danced ev'-ry dance and I walked you back home, so long a-go, but I want you to know that I'm still so in love with you.

37
cresc.
Ooh,
cresc.
41
I re - mem - ber the night when I
45
knew you were mine, by the soft can - dle - light we both

tast - ed the wine, on a night just like this, love was sealed with a kiss, and all my dreams came true. There were times when we laughed, there were times when we cried, there were times when we thought that our love must have died, well you're here with me now, guess we made it some-how, and I'm still so in love with you. After all the years,

af-ter all the tears, yes, I'm still so in love with you.

Ooh.

THE GREAT GNOME ROBBERY

Text: Myles Rudge
Music: Mike Sammes

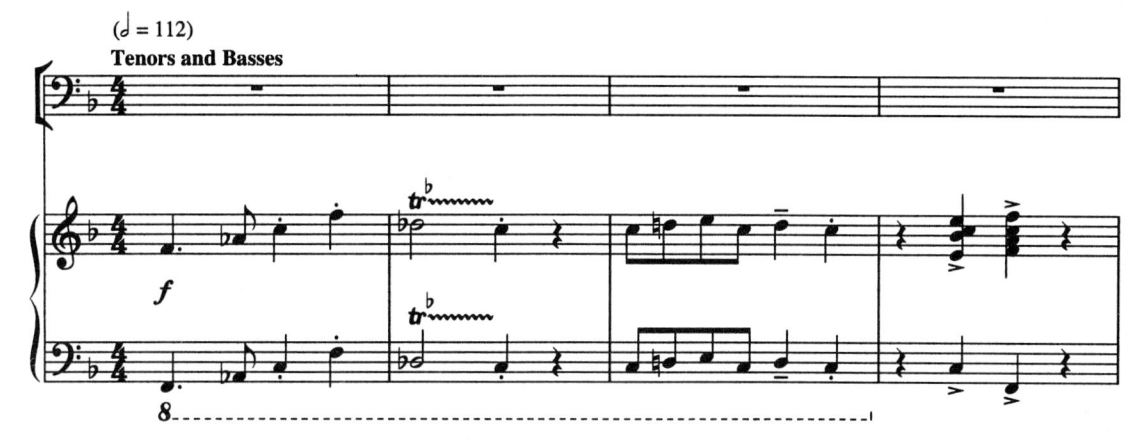

(♩ = 112)
Tenors and Basses

We'd been out, when we got home some-bo-dy had nicked our gar-den gnome, rot-ten, mean thing to do, they took his lit-tle toad-stool too. The

© Copyright Cyril Shane Music Ltd, Suite 8, Westwood House, 123 Westmead Road, Sutton, Surrey SM1 4JH. Reproduced by permission.
It is illegal to photocopy music.

Ooh, wife was ve-ry sha-ken up in-deed,

'Oh my Gawd!' Ooh, she said, and I a-greed!

Some are made of plas-tic, and some are made of stone,

some have lit-tle gno-mey friends, and some are all a-lone, but a gar-den's not a gar-den, and a house is not a home, un-less you've got a gar-den gnome to call your ve-ry own.

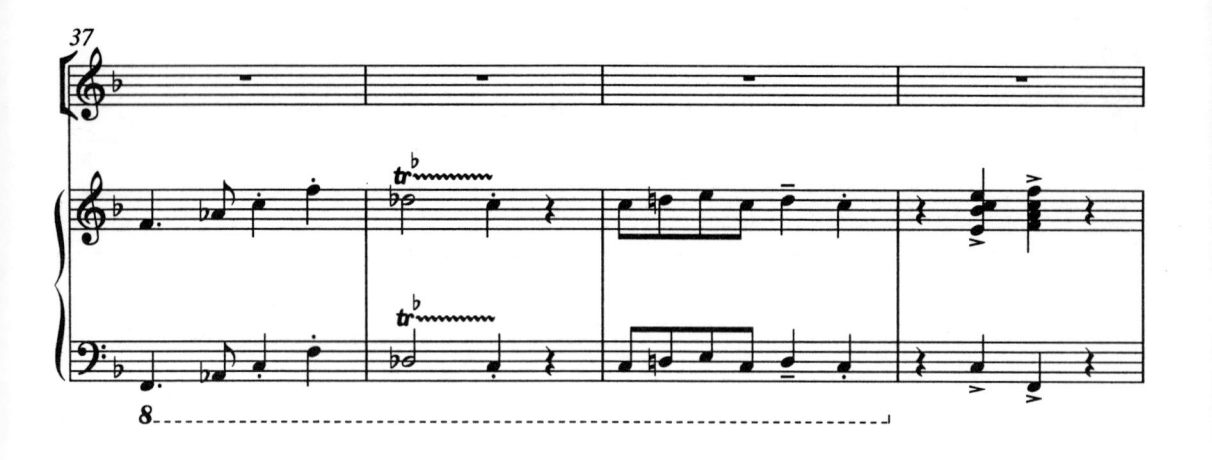

Searched a-round but found no trace, no-thing but an emp-ty gnome-less space, so to e-ven up the score I pinched one from the

Ooh, house next door. I told the wife, 'They've more gnomes than they need!', 'Oh my Gawd!' Ooh, she said, and I a-greed! Some are made of plas-tic, and some are made of stone, some have lit-tle gno-mey friends, and some are all a-lone, but a gar-den's not a gar - den, and a house is not a home, un-less you've got a gar - den gnome to call your ve-ry own!

Went to bed quite chuffed be-cause we'd got a ni-cer gnome than our gnome was, but next day, strange but true, ours was back so now we've two! Ooh, I asked the wife, 'Sup-

'Oh, my Gawd!' she po-sing they should breed?' said, and I a-greed! Ooh, Some are made of plas-tic, and some are made of stone, some have lit-tle gno-mey friends, and

(2nd time - have fun)

gliss.

some are all a-lone, but a gar-den's not a gar - den, and a

house is not a home un - less you've got a gar - den gnome to call

your ve-ry own! Yes, However far you

rubato

wander, how-e-ver far you roam, how-e-ver ma-ny gnomes you find, there's no gnome like your own. Ours is a nice gnome, ours is!

colla voce

a tempo

VERSATILITY

(A Cappella)
Text and music: Mike Sammes

We can sing in E flat, it's a love-ly key, or if you pre-fer it we can sing in B. We still pre-fer E flat, but it goes too high, so we'll take it down a notch; I'll tell you why. D ma-jor is a

© Copyright 1996 Kevin Mayhew Ltd.
It is illegal to photocopy music.

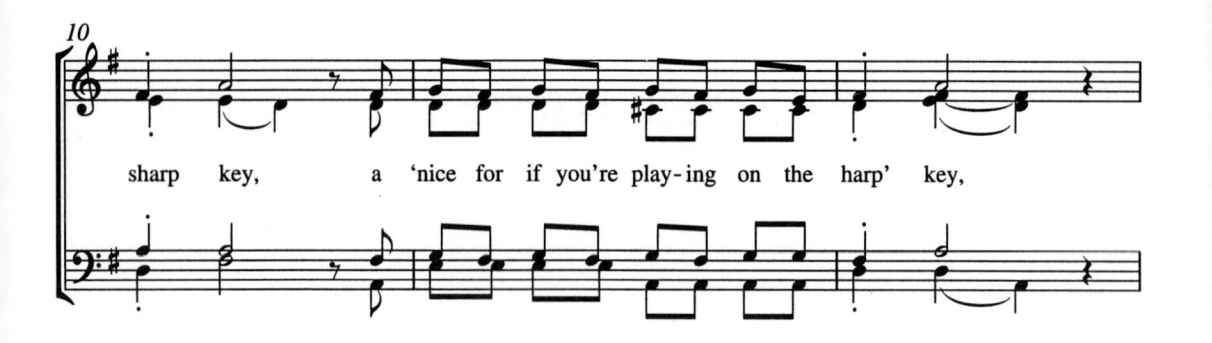

sharp key, a 'nice for if you're play-ing on the harp' key,

and it's sim-ple, you see, to shift in-to the key of

E. We can sing in A flat, and some-times in a

house! We can sing Burt Bach-er-ach or

dear, oh dear! *(Feel of A major)*

* *One voice, spoken resignedly - probably the conductor.*

e - ven Jo - hann Strauss.
pa pa pa pa pa. But here we go a-gain now,
Oom, oom, oom.

eyes down, look-ing in, back to where we start-ed, it's a fla - ming sin,

we can sing in E flat, we hope ve - ry soon to re-port that we can sing in

E in tune! Doh, re, me, so far, so good!

HUMMING BIRD

Mike Sammes

47

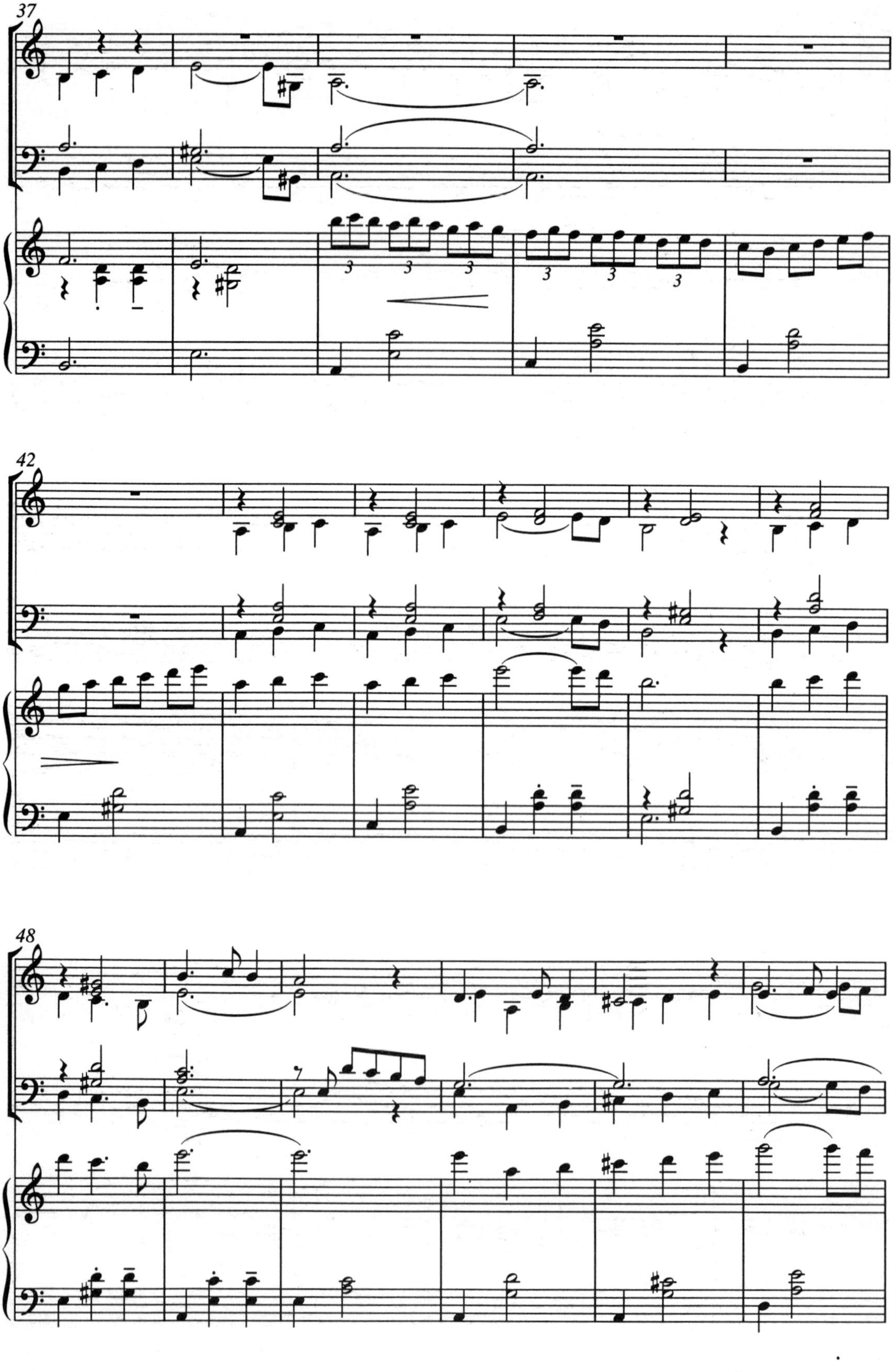
37
42
48

49

50

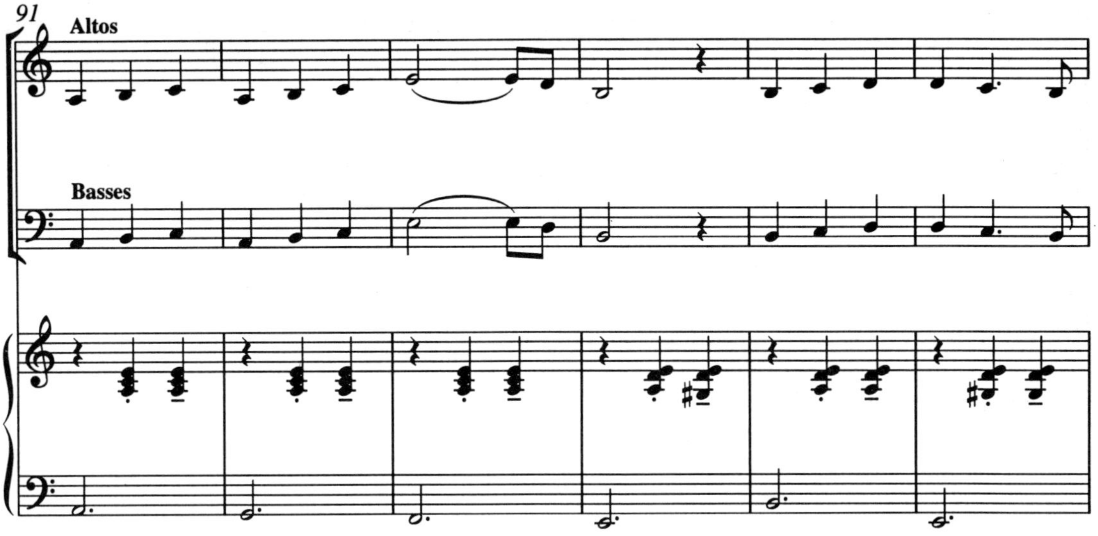
91
Altos
Basses

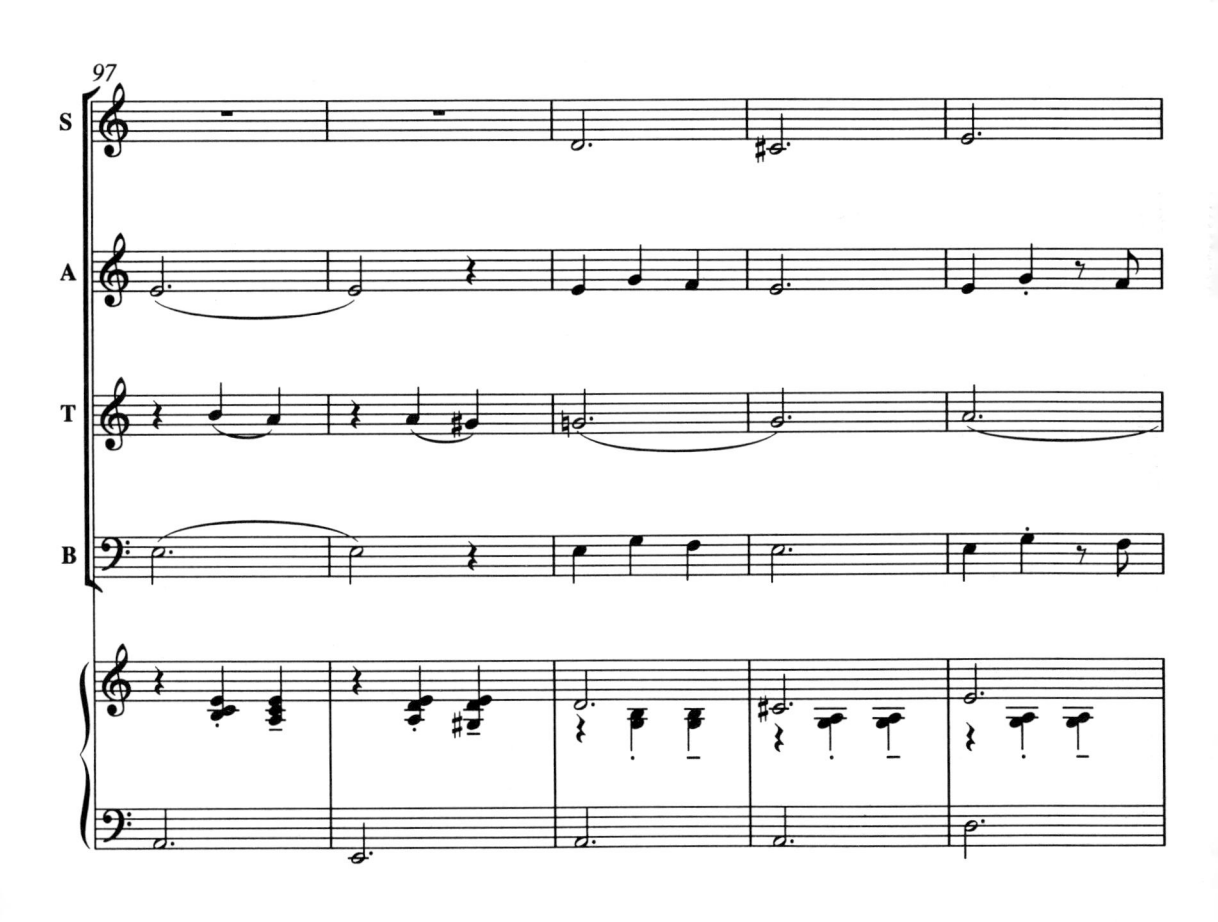
97
S
A
T
B

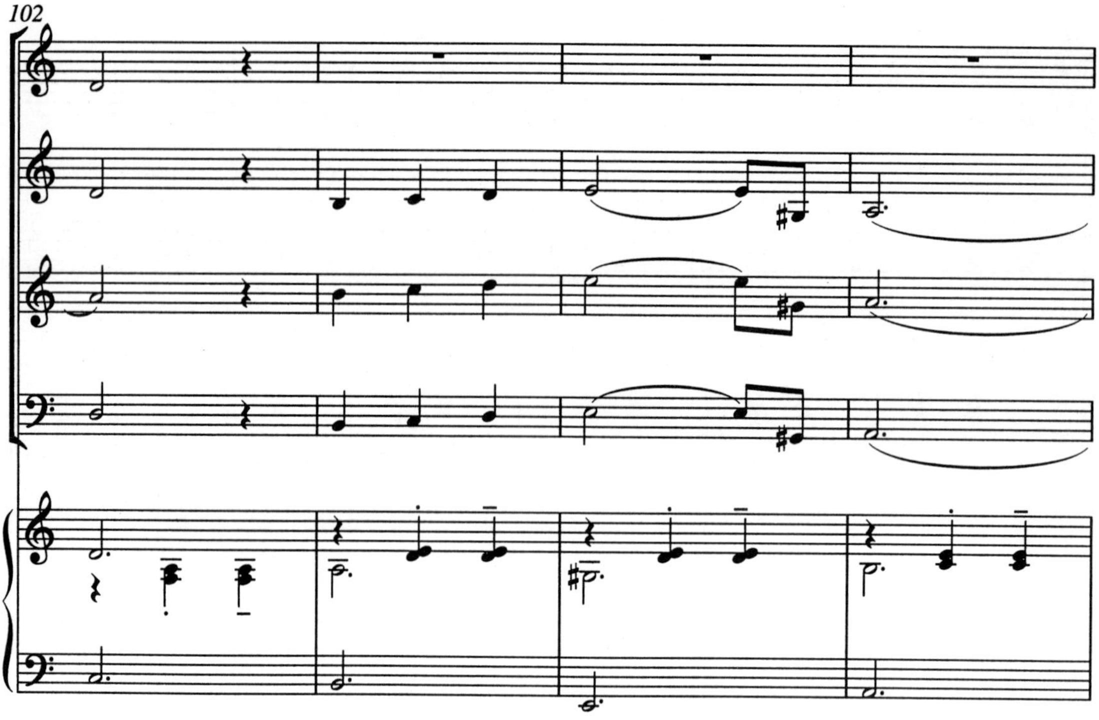
102

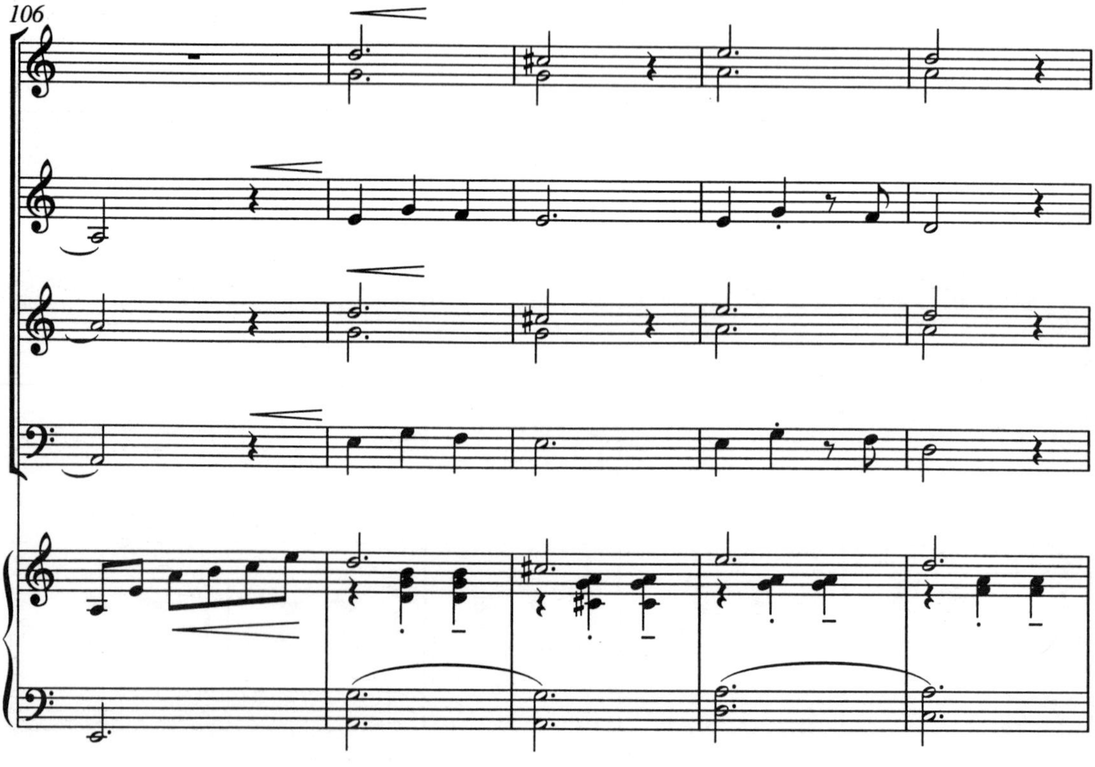
106

53

COMIN' THROUGH THE RYE

Text: Traditional Scottish
Music: Traditional Scottish Melody arranged by Mike Sammes

Swing a bit!

A - hum, a - hum, a - hum, a - hum, a - hum, a-

If a bo-dy meet a bo-dy co-min' through the rye,

hum, a - hum, a - hum, a-

* Play dotted rhythm as triplets

© Copyright 1996 Kevin Mayhew Ltd.
It is illegal to photocopy music.

10
if a bo-dy greet a bo-dy, need a bo-dy
hum, a - hum, a - hum, a - hum, a -
14
cry? Ev - 'ry las-sie has her lad-die,
hum.
sim.
17
ne'er a one have I, but all the lads they smile at me when

21
3
co - min' through the rye. Do be dt, do be dt, do be do be do - ee - ood'n
24
3
dt do be dt, do be dt, do be do be do - ee - ood' n dp.
If a bo - dy
27
do dp do dp
meet a bo - dy co - min' from the well,

30
if a bo - dy kiss a bo - dy, need a bo - dy
33
Ev - 'ry las - sie has her lad - die,
tell?
36
ne'er a one have I, but all the lads they
do dt do do dp do dp

smile at me when co-min' through the rye.
do do do, a-hum, a-
hum, a-hum, a-
hum.
Rubato
If a bo-dy meet a bo-dy

47
co - min' from the town, if a bo - dy
mp
50
kiss a bo - dy, need a bo - dy frown?
53
Ev - 'ry las - sie has her lad - die, ne'er a one have
do, do, do, do,
do,
Do, do,
3
3

I, but all the lads they smile at me when co-min' through the rye.

Rye, through the rye, through the rye, do be do be do-ee-ood' n, dt do be dt do be

If a bo-dy

Tempo I

68
meet a bo- dy co - min' through the rye,
dt do be do be do-ee-ood' n, dt do be dt do be
70
if a bo - dy
dt do be do be do - ee - ood' n, dt do be dt do be
72
greet a bo - dy need a bo - dy
dt do be do be do - ee - ood' n, dt do be dt do be

cry? Ev' - ry las - sie

dt do be do be do - ee - ood' n.

has her lad - die, ne'er a one have I, but

all the lads they smile at me when co - min'

through the rye, through the rye, through the rye, do be dt, do be dt, do be do be do-ee-oo-d'n dt, de oo be do be do be dt dt do yup!

THE KERRY DANCE

Text: Traditional Irish
Music: Traditional Irish Melody arranged by Mike Sammes

Oh, the days of the Ker - ry danc - ing, oh, the ring of the pi - per's tune,

Slower

oh, for one of those hours of glad - ness, gone, a - las, like our youth too

Rhythmically (♩ = 132)

soon. When the boys be - gan to ga - ther in the glen of a

© Copyright 1996 Kevin Mayhew Ltd.
It is illegal to photocopy music.

sum - mer night, and the Ker-ry Pi - per's tun - ing made us long -

with wild de - light!- Oh, to think of it,

oh, to dream of it fills my heart with tears,

oh, the days of the Ker - ry danc - ing, oh, the ring of the pi - per's tune, oh, for one of those hours of glad - ness, gone, a - las, like our youth too soon.

Was there e-ver a sweet-er col-leen in the dance than Ei-ly Moore, or a proud-er lad than Tha-dy as he bold-ly took-a the floor? Lads and las-ses, all to your plac-es, up the mid-dle and down a-gain,

legato

ah, the mer - ry - heart - ed laugh - ter, ring - ing

through the hap - py glen!

rubato

Oh, to think of it, oh, to dream of it, fills my heart with

tears. Oh, the days of the Ker-ry dan-cing, oh, the ring of the pi-per's tune, oh, for one of those hours of glad-ness, gone, a-las, like our youth

65
too soon.
it's gone, it's gone
68
Oh, for one of those
72
rit.
f
hours of glad - ness, gone, all gone!

Gone, a-las, like our youth too soon,

too soon, too soon.

(nn)

A LITTLE KNOWLEDGE

Text: Bill Owen
Music: Mike Sammes

© Copyright Pedro Music Ltd, rights assigned to Cyril Shane Music Ltd, Suite 8, Westmead House, 123 Westmead Road, Sutton, Surrey SM1 4JH. Reproduced by permission.
It is illegal to photocopy music.

dt. Do, ooh, he just stood and stared, but then he got quite per-plexed when the li-on licked his lips. He whis-pered, 'What do I do next?' A lit-tle know-ledge is a dan-ger-ous thing, such a dan-ger-ous

thing, a lit-tle know-ledge is a dan-ger-ous thing, oh, what trou-ble it can bring! A pig once made some wings be-cause he'd heard, if pigs could fly, then

a-ny-thing could hap-pen, so he leapt right up in-to the sky, but little pigs are fat and no mat-ter how he tried, he boo hoo, ooh, flapped his arms to no a-vail and then sat down and cried. A lit-tle

know-ledge is a dan-ger-ous thing, such a dan-ger-ous thing, a lit-tle know-ledge is a dan-ger-ous thing, oh, what trou-ble it can bring. Oh, what a dan-ger-ous thing, a dan-ger-ous thing of which I do sing, oh, what a dan-ger-ous thing,

let me tell you more: A ba-by hip-po-po-ta-mus said:

'How I'd like to swim!', like fish-es do,
he thought he knew, 'cos

they were all less big than him. He dived from off the bank, but that was the end of that, 'cos he was down the shal-low end, that's why his nose is flat! A lit-tle know-ledge is a dan-ger-ous thing, such a dan-ger-ous thing, a lit-tle know-ledge is a dan-ger-ous thing, oh, what trou-ble it can bring! A lit-tle bring!

Dt, do, dt, do!
Do, dt, do, dt, dt, do!

SOLDIER, SOLDIER

Text: Traditional English
Music: Traditional English Melody arranged by Mike Sammes

*Male voices roll the 'r's like a drum sound

© Copyright 1996 Kevin Mayhew Ltd.
It is illegal to photocopy music.

12
no, pret-ty maid, I can-not mar-ry you, for I have no coat to put on, to put on, for I
16
Ah, ooh.
have no coat to put on.
So
20
off to the tai - lor she did go as fast as she could run,

and she bought him a coat from a tailor of note and the sol-dier put it on, it on, and the sol-dier put it on.

Oh sol-dier, sol-dier, will you mar-ry me, with your

musket, fife and drum? drum, rrum. Oh no, pretty maid, I cannot marry you, for I have no pants to put on, to put on, for I have no pants to put on. So back to the tailor she did go as fast as she could run, and she bought him a pair of the finest there and the soldier put them on, them on, and the

58
Oh
sol - dier put them on.
61
sol - dier, sol - dier, will you mar - ry me, with your mus - ket, fife and drum?
rrum, rrum, rrum, rrum,
65
rrum. Oh no, pret - ty maid, I can - not mar - ry you, for I have no shoes to put

on, to put on, for I have no shoes to put on. Ah, ooh,

So off to the cob-blers she did go as fast as she could

run, run, run,

run,

80

(S/A): run,

(T): and she bought him a pair of the fin-est there and the

(B): and she bought him a pair of the fin-est there and the

83

(T): sol-dier put them on, them on, and the sol-dier put them on.

(B): sol-dier put them on, them on, and the sol-dier put them on.

87

(S/A): Oh sol-dier, sol-dier, will you mar-ry me, with your mus-ket, fife and

(T/B): rrum, rrum, rrum,

91
drum?
rrum, rrum. Oh no, pret-ty maid, I can-not mar-ry you, for I
95
Ooh, ooh, ooh, ah,
have no hat to put on, to put on, for I have no hat to put on.
99
ooh. So off to the hat - ter she did go as

fast as she could run, run, run,

and she bought him a hat, a fine silk hat, and the sol-dier put it on,

it on, and the sol-dier put it on. **Sopranos and Altos** Now sol-dier, sol-dier, will you mar-ry me, with your mus-ket, fife and drum?

rrum, rrum, rrum, rrum,

Ooh,

Ooh,

rrum. Oh no, pret-ty maid, I can-not mar-ry you, I've a

rrum. Ooh, I've a

123
wife and a ba - by at home, at home, I've a wife and a ba - by
wife and a ba - by at home, at home, I've a wife and a ba - by

126
Do do be do be dt, do - dt!
Do do be do be dt, do - dt!
at home, do dt!
at home, do dt!

THE VIRGIN MARY

Text: Traditional West Indian
Music: Traditional West Indian Melody arranged by Mike Sammes

© Copyright 1996 Kevin Mayhew Ltd.
It is illegal to photocopy music.

11
S
A
T
B
gave him the name of Je - sus.
He come from the glo - ry,
15
he come from the glo - ri - ous a - king - dom.
Oh,
18
yes, be - lie - ver,
oh,
yes, be - lie - ver,

he come from the glo - ry, he come from the glo-ri-ous a-king-dom.

The wise men saw when the ba-by born, the

wise men saw where the ba-by born, the wise men went where the ba-by born and they said that his name was Je-sus. He come from the glo-ry, he come from the glo-ri-ous a-king-dom. Oh,

43
yes, be-lie - ver, oh, yes, be-lie - ver,
47
he come from the glo - ry, he come from the glo-ri-ous a-king-dom.
51
Hmm.